Influences:

The *Irish* Poems

poems by

Karen Petersen

Finishing Line Press
Georgetown, Kentucky

"We'll meet again, we'll part once more."
James Joyce, Finnegans Wake

Influences:

The *Irish* Poems

Copyright © 2025 by Karen Petersen
ISBN 979-8-89990-097-6 First Edition
All rights reserved under International and Pan-American Copyright Conventions. No part of this book may be reproduced in any manner whatsoever without written permission from the publisher, except in the case of brief quotations embodied in critical articles and reviews.

ACKNOWLEDGMENTS

A New Ulster: "In Memory of Seamus Heaney;" "Remembering Paddy's Market, Glasgow;" "Galway Viriditas;" "The Whooper Swans of Fermangh;" "For My Late Friend, Who I Knew for 52 Years;" "Excuses for Idleness No. 137: Counting Pennies;" "Noah's Ark;" "Elegy for Kate (Karin);" "The Long Night's Moon Has Come (Short-listed for the Foley Poetry Prize);" "In Memory of W.B. Yeats;" "Counting Down ("Three Poems from the Time of the Pandemic")"
The Journal of Undiscovered Poets: "A Vacation in Wales, After the War"
The Malpais Review: "Glenna"
The Bosphorus Review of Books: "Ten Years"

With Special Thanks to Louis De Santis.

Publisher: Leah Huete de Maines
Editor: Christen Kincaid
Cover Art: The Book of Kells, Trinity College, Dublin
Author Photo: Louis De Santis
Cover Design: Elizabeth Maines McCleavy

Order online: www.finishinglinepress.com
also available on amazon.com and barnesandnoble.com

Author inquiries and mail orders:
Finishing Line Press
PO Box 1626
Georgetown, Kentucky 40324
USA

Contents

Introduction ix
In Memory of Seamus Heaney 1
Remembering Paddy's Market, Glasgow 2
Galway Viriditas 4
Glenna 5
The Whooper Swans of Fermangh 6
The Habits of a Landscape 7
For My Late Friend Who I Knew for 52 Years 8
A Vacation in Wales, After the War 9
Fernie 10
Excuses for Idleness No. 137: Counting Pennies 11
Looking for the Perseid Meteor Shower 12
Noah's Ark 14
First Love 15
Ten Years 16
The Hat 17
Elegy for Kate 18
Prologue 19
The Long Night's Moon Has Come 20
War & Peace 21
Write What You Would Never Say 22
The Mirrored Gaze 23
Lineages 24
Epistolary 25
Crossing a Field 26
Counting Down 27
The Three Cats of Tobermory 28
The Small Things 29
The Brightness of Leaving 30
A Summer Accident 31
In Memory of W.B. Yeats 32

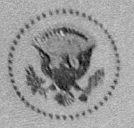

THE WHITE HOUSE
WASHINGTON

June 10, 2024

Ms. Karen Petersen
Santa Fe, New Mexico

Dear Ms. Petersen,

I love poetry—thank you for sharing yours with me. One of my favorite contemporary poets, Seamus Heaney, wrote in his 1991 work The Cure at Troy:

> History says, "Don't hope
> On this side of the grave."
> But then, once in a lifetime
> the longed-for tidal wave
> of justice can rise up,
> and hope and history rhyme.

Though we as a Nation have lived through some of our most difficult days, I truly believe in the bright future ahead. Together, let's make hope and history rhyme.

Sincerely,

Joe Biden

Introduction

President Biden was a well-known fan of Irish poets, especially the late, great Seamus Heaney. Many of my poems of a certain ilk have been published in the two Irelands, and recently gathered into this chapbook called *Influences: The* Irish *Poems*. So during the presidential campaign trail in early 2024 I thought it might be something he might enjoy while on the road. So I sent it off with a short note but did not really expect a response.

In the ensuing weeks I forgot all about it. However, when I first saw the White House envelope on expensive Crane stationery in my mail one day I almost threw it out, thinking it was some kind of fancy fund-raising letter, but then I thought better, and opened it...hah!

In Memory of Seamus Heaney:
Reef the sails. Batten down.

Wind-tipped, then wind-drunk
up went the sails into a fine billow
my crow's nest of a life
in full world-tilt
as the rolling waves carried us out
past the flat clean sandbars, with their shoals
and eddies of tiny silver fish darting about.
"Where to?" I asked,
and the Captain replied "Anywhere is fine"
so we headed West, deep water
almost obsidian-black now, surface-hard,
whose unfathomable depths
summoned an unseen underworld.
I couldn't gaze upon that;
it felt like the very darkest reaches,
like the day my brother died
so I looked out and beyond
as the setting sun bathed the sky
in washes of soft color:
"open now as the eye of heaven,"
and the world became gentle again.

Remembering Paddy's Market, Glasgow

When I was young, my grandmother
would frequently look at my bedroom,
which was usually in a state of chassis,
and exclaim, "It's like Paddy's Market in here."
But it wasn't until I was older and got to travel
that I saw the actual wondrous space,
a true sign of the times, a "crime-ridden midden"
according to the nervous local council,
filled with the flotsam and jetsam of lives
now abandoned or in desperate enough need
for a few quid or perhaps just the attention
gotten from putting out your best shoes for sale.

"Four fur a fiver," one merchant cried,
her wee stall tucked under a railway arch
in the lane running between the city center
and the River Clyde. Her clothes, books and
furniture were strewn along two rickety tables
and a camp-bed, upon which sat a friend
who'd stopped by for a morning chat.
"I got my first two-tone suit here
when I was a Mod years ago," he said,
flicking the ash of his cigarette
off onto the grey, ancient pavement.

Around for over two hundred years
the market met its demise in May of '09,
and with it went the second-hand fur coats,
mismatched shoes, guitars and cuddly toys.
Run by generations of working class Irish,
the hawkers seemed bemused or resigned;
after all, this end was nothing compared
to the Great Hunger of 1845, the real end.
The lane is quiet now, the shops gone,
Empty except for the pigeon flocks
and the echoes of an old man's words
to the tv crew on the market's last day...
"I dunna think we'll have anywhere to go na
because Glasgow's gettin' too posh."

Galway Viriditas

They called me a bogtrotter and
a culchie, but what did they know?
missing the Mysteries of the land they were
the Amen of the full moon
whose light cleansed and blessed us all;
even the blind could find their way to Heaven.

Tourists come now to look at the pretty view
but the land is silent
and they don't know what they're seein':
the past where starvation lay, where a boy of 10
vanished over a 5 cent candy bar...Amen.
And where was the church then? Asleep on a pew.

Do you know the comfort the rain
brings to our tears
as we stand silently in the wood?
What would the world be, bereft of wildness,
bereft of places of deep viriditas.
These are our chapels. Amen.

"Solvitur ambulando," down corcach paths
hemmed by the singing insects of summer and
open to the clarity of silver sea & cloud-scud:
We resonate with the small, in awe of the large,
seascape to landscape to homescape to grave
this world is Paradise enough.

Glenna

The magnolia, planted
after my grandmother's death
in her honor,
was acting up again,
its petals fallen on the ground like so many tears.
I watered it, pruned it, admired it
what more did it want from me?

My grandmother had lived far away,
in Canada,
a little old lady with a straw handbag
from a cruise to Bermuda.
Of Scottish decent,
she carried all the baggage
that went with that.

She was thrifty and reserved.
Her passions came out in her baking:
lemon tart, fruitcake, sweet rolls.
Seductive rolls like pillows,
frisky tarts, moist and inviting,
complex fruitcakes, gastronomic labyrinths.
Extravagant things.

I ignored her most of the time
except at Christmas when the baked goods came,
in a small parcel with a customs sticker on it.
So then she was with us, like the host
eaten at Mass. And now this tree
is there, part of the daily ordinary,
reminding me to pay attention.

The Whooper Swans of Fermanagh
(a found poem—with thanks to Dara McAnulty)

*"Out with you upon the wild waves, Children of the King!
Henceforth your cries shall be with the flocks of birds."*

It was like any other day in the forest
until we saw them, all four;
they could have been the children of Lir:
Fionnuala, Aodh, Fiachra and Conn,
from Irish legend, whooper swans,
ancient travelers, they landed
gracefully on the silver-lit lake
long white necks held high,
and stayed with us a long time.
Suddenly the honking and trumpeting began;
their wild cries, without abandon and yet forlorn,
were joyous and magnificent.
As we reverently watched
I felt magic in the air,
and wings extending on the leader swan,
heads bobbed and rose as they
all communicated, ready for flight,
as throughout the centuries
they soared off Northwesterly—
perhaps towards Iceland, past the tolling
bells of the old stone monasteries,
and into the bright clouds.

The Habits of a Landscape
for Robert Macfarlane

Seeking shelter from the darkening landscape,
restless storms on the horizon, maybe a squall,
I had walked into a sunken path, harrowed deep
from many years of wheel-run & foot-fret,
when the hail began, thump-thumping the ground,
tearing the tender leaves newly emerged
on this early Spring afternoon.

The hail ended and all was quiet, recovering,
and I came out onto bright fields, all golden and
trembling from the wind as it headed north
towards the blustery colder regions.
A small nest of quail, startled and vulnerable,
was hidden in the interior of a double hedge
so I walked on pretending not to notice them.

On the nearby pond was a paddle of ducks,
all around them the grasses going silver in the wind,
and the pond going silver in the sun—and suddenly
I'm blinded by this ecstatic light of the Godhead.
These small transcendent moments are Nature's
gift to us, we the onlookers, the humble participants,
only just out for an afternoon walk in the old dale.

Still air, hard frost, deep quiet, greet me now
Moon-shadows embracing old stagheads
staking their archaic claim on the heath amid
this aching wonder of silence and solitude.
Meandering hills hide their age in soft curves,
ancient paths speak of use, both human and wild.
The language of Nature is everywhere.

For My Late Friend, Who I Knew For 52 Years

Last night I finally saw you again, in a dream,
in a great hall at Oxford, inexplicably,
since neither of us went there
—though your mother was Irish, your fragile,
beautiful mother who you take so much after.
Although you are gone forever from this Earth,
what a gift to lay eyes on you and talk like old times
even if you were clearly ill and pale, you were present,
smiling at me, one more time.
There you were, working on something in your studious way
and as you looked up I knew I was gazing on someone
who was not long for this world, and I woke up crying.
Crying out of gratitude tho', because
you came to me one last time, and that was special,
although it was clear that in that world too,
you did not have much time.
Our dreams are ephemeral but they allow us a passage
and a chance to dwell, albeit briefly, in the fullness of love
with one whom we miss very much.
While the nightmares of Hieronymus lurk in the shadows
they do not dare to come out, the light is so strong,
the light is so strong.

A Vacation in Wales, After the War

It was all glowing pink, purple and green
on the small hills above the house today,
the heather and gorse almost on fire
with their fierce, wind-spangled colors.
Geese overhead at dawn, charms of goldfinches
in the privet, the far summits standing clear.
We had a fast sunlit race across the moors,
cloud-shadows flowing over the fells, swallows
hunting low through the flower meadows.
And as I ran across the old chalk finish line
behind my brother, no longer wee but all grown now,
a man in full, I stumbled and he gathered me up,
safe and unhurt, as if I was still a young lass.
To be surrounded by family and unfettered landscape
today was a kind of bountiful perfection, and gave
some peace amid the clattering and hammering
of my troubled dreams, hiding away in a far-off place.

Fernie
for the late Oliver Sacks

Delicate and moisture loving,
tough enough to sprout
on a hardscrabble lava flow,
my fernie is a great opportunist
—a green Santa run amok—
filling the air with millions of
spores from miniature sacks,
even when all else is extinct.

Lover of chinks, crevices,
old crumbling mortar,
dry desert, and shadowy glades,
my fronded fernie
can live a hundred years,
when circumstances permit.

As big as twelve feet or
smaller than a baby's toe,
Spring green, blue, or black,
roaming, creeping, climbing,
whisktail, fiddlehead, or ostrich,
I'm sure my fulsome fernie
will be cavorting about
long after I am humus.

Excuses for Idleness no. 137: Counting Pennies

My grandmother would visit the UK often
and upon her much anticipated return she'd
press into my hand some pennies for candy,
back when those sweet delights cost little.
These old pennies were proper things.
A good size, a good weight, a good solid base
on which to build a pound sterling one day.
There was Britannia, secure behind her shield,
holding out an olive branch, with or without
a lighthouse in the background, and
there was possibly even the young Victoria
on the other side, with ribbons in her hair.

I learned you could sew pennies into the hem
of a wide skirt so it wouldn't blow up in the wind
and there were some curtains at school with weights
in the corners that I was convinced were pennies.
One year I remember still being very small and
in possession of unimaginable riches: half a crown!
My mother took me to the bank and when I was given
the exchange I had even more. Coins and coins
and coins! Copper and silver! Too much to hold…
But my mother explained to me
how "more could mean less,"
and I've been a cynic ever since.

Looking for the Perseid Meteor Shower

I felt a bit foolish
standing outside
the front of my house
in my nightgown
staring up at the heavens
at 3 in the morning.
It was the Perseids
I'd hoped to see;
the only person on my block
awake at that time.
I wanted some signal
from the heavens
and stood there, mouth agape,
tilting back, nearly falling over,
looking at the darkness
with all its glittering beauty.
Perhaps some of the space dust,
microscopic,
from the many comets
would rain down on me
and I thought of my late mother
and wondered if a few of her
molecules had come from space
to be with me again:
perhaps Mozart too, and
many other people from
the last several thousand years.

They would all be covering me
in a space cloak of humanity
on that dark suburban street.
There was a bright comet I saw,
others were very small
and teased the corner of my eye,
and when I looked
they were already gone,
but I did catch that one;
a large radiant flare
streaking across the Milky Way,
and I'd like to think
it was the Universe waving.

Noah's Ark

I love the story of Noah and the Ark
mainly because you can twist it around
and still maintain the essence of the story.
It could be sci-fi, or it could possibly be
some crazy Middle Eastern guy
holed up in a boat, drunk and stranded,
at the edge of a vast desert.
You can tell it straight as a myth or go for realism,
basically do anything you want
and still remain true to the ancient story.

I hope Noah put the dinosaurs in the bottom
or the whole thing would have tipped over.
Always wondered about the insects...
and the presence of those lurking vultures
is too painful to contemplate.
In the old manuscript drawings,
is that a pie on the top deck?
Was there anything in Genesis
about Noah saving a pie??
My feeling is that it may be a grain store,
though I like the idea that he saved
the blackbirds by hiding them in a pie.

First Love

He was just a boy in my arms
wanting to be a man
on sunlit cliffs whose heights
broached no danger, only the lingering
salt of the sea and where
two lovers
in their first embrace
no minute, no hour could console;
so easily led to happiness
but like quicksilver
he was just a boy
wanting to be a man
wanting to be a boy.

Ten Years

Ten years after my father's death
my mother looks at his photo
and says she cannot
even remember his voice.
She's forgotten—or is it pain?—
the strange depths of their last
ten years together: the light
and the dark.
So it is I,
the umbilical thread,
that holds it all together now;
the frayed, fraying, gossamer fineness
of memory, my only inheritance.
See? I am the keeper, I am the tomb.

The Hat

It started innocently enough:
small gestures, smiles,
flirting was fun and
made me feel attractive
although I'm of a certain age.

I was wearing a hat,
it covered my hair,
graying at the roots and
without it I looked
my age, but with it on

the years rolled back
to an almost kind of
youth, and freedom,
with playful eyes full
of promise and seduction.

Then with a nod to Fate
the hat slid off
and there I was, revealed,
and the room froze,
the elderly had come.

There was a sense of shock,
of shame, and finally,
disgust. I tried to smile
but was met with hostility:
the interloper in a hat,
quite invisible now.

Elegy for Kate

Gone when the leaves turned
on a half-moon Fall night
"She's passed," her friend said,
his emotions hanging on a thread
of cold autumn air.
When she went we whispered
she left us a little frailer,
missing her unique song,
although just around the corner
her spirit which fluttered in the light
still flutters there, a quiet thing.

Prologue

The time has come to shut the door.
Colder nights, shorter days,
a hurried sky and placid light.
I take the heat from the ashes
as the fire dims
and stand alone to watch
the shifting tenses of the hours
amid a multitude of wildflowers
—soon blown away to nothing
by a hardscrabble wind.
In measured ways I live,
lapse and relapse,
yielding only to time
and staked earth;
the rock-floored bed awaits,
a tender sleep among the leaves.

The Long Night's Moon Has Come

I wander the world dwelling in one
dark blue eventide after another,
frequenting mountains, caves, forests
and other lonely places,
where hunting sparrow hawks send
small birds shattering out of branches
and into the mouths of waiting foxes.

Sometimes the sky brightly glitters in parts
while being ominously dark in others, often
foretelling storm, rain or snow:
fine, wind-driven snow disorienting and
obscuring the northern stars so I lose my way,
or 'dog's-feet-snow' falling in large flakes,
quickly blanketing the landscape
and freezing even the shadows under the trees.

I look sunward to feel its warmth on my face,
its apricity, and remember the shimmering
eldritch mirages of the brutal heat
in the southern latitudes
destroying all equilibrium and sanity.
I just want to close my eyes and sleep now
or else shout my regrets at the lone skylark
riding the currents of all that emptiness.

And then there is this moon
glowing and round, strong light flowing
like a river through the night sky
a giant portal to the heavens.
I lean back, conquered, defenseless,
surrendered in full, completely subsumed
until that delicate pink blush above the horizon
arrives, with its beautiful wild edges.

War & Peace

These green hills, so soft and welcoming,
hide all manner of treachery and sadness.
Their grassy bosoms caress the dead,
buried deeply down in the timeless dark,
unquiet mouths trying to speak in vain
above the wind rolling in from the rippling sea.

Below those waters, in fields of sea grass,
a platoon of arms wave in macabre choreography,
waving goodbye to life, goodbye, goodbye,
yet above, on the shore, it's just another sunny day
of strollers, lovers, and happy oblivion.
And why not, the dead don't rise.

Write What You Would Never Say
in memory of Denis Johnson

I left those mean NY streets
a long time ago.
I made the choice after
lying in bed one night, hair sticky with rum,
heart beating like a triphammer.

Too much clubbing and drugging,
did I want the humiliation of the ER?
So I stayed, fighting it, calming down slowly.
Are you serious?
—*This exhaustion mutilated to resemble passion.*
It was that kind of twisted decade.

Heard my now departed neighbor
had drowned all her kittens
and then vanished,
leaving the building with
fucked up plumbing.

She'd been from the Midwest.
Overwhelmed, she'd crept off into the full moon.
Probably a suicide in the luminous river.
Tired now of all the tramps
gleefully wagging their limp dicks
on the corner of 39th and 8th Ave.

Tourists staring in shock,
locals oblivious.
The sky is yellow at 3 a.m.
The sounds of traffic not quite gone,
it's almost tranquil, this grave.

The Mirrored Gaze

I'm reading some poems
on the death of a badger,
the stillbirth of a lamb,
a trapped rat—all brutal and dazzling.
But we can't, really,
keep with us
the true horrors of the world,
unless we stumble upon them
by accident.
It's just too much.

The misshapen crushed skulls,
the smeared blood-meat on the road,
the agony of disease.
All the quiet ruinations.
To try and hold that in place,
simultaneously,
with the beauty of the world,
seems almost impossible
on this sunny, blue sky day
here in County Wexford.

I try and contemplate
the other side of the mirror,
to hold it with me
but I look away,
gazing dumbly at the wall
of my house, to think instead:
it's time to prune
those tree branches away
before they damage the stucco.
It's all I can manage.

Lineages

If a wedding dress could only speak the things it would say.

My great Aunt's long silk dress from the early 1900s was scary:
wasp waist, large bosom, demurely placed shoulder straps
to show off the diamonds, a hint of lace peeking out
from the bottom to titillate the one who would have her later,
and all those who wouldn't.
Their Darien reception was sedate and dignified,
and they left for their Palm Beach honeymoon in a Bentley.

My mother, practical to the end, got married
in a well-tailored suit with a large orchid corsage on her lapel,
and a great pair of high heels. Her legs were worthy
of Betty Grable, and it was just after the war.
Their wild D.C. reception had lots of soldiers and secretaries
and they left for their Catskills honeymoon
on a shiny, new BMW motorcycle.

My dress was a short, beautifully embroidered cotton dress
faithfully sewn by Mexican peasant women under the hot sun
only to be left in my closet,
forlorn and eventually forgotten, finally returned to the store
after all hope had been abandoned. I cried that day,
but only for the end of a dream. That night I left on the train
to go back to the city, and a big job--it was enough.

Epistolary
for James Finnegan

Her nouns were real.
Her nouns were sighs.
They rose in the air
like lullabies.
That Sunday afternoon
she set her trap
from innocent dreams,
and discarded vows,
rising,
rising now.
Her verbs were real.
Her verbs were cruel.
Arabesques of pain,
finely wrought jewels.
We parted in silence
angry shadows, interrupted,
and the afternoon grieved,
undone, and corrupted.

Crossing a Field

Crossing a field at midnight,
restless, I blunder into
the stirring stillness of a herd,
its dark force and mass
in the night-thickness
holding the land down by their presence.
I feel their heat, tatters of hay
frittering towards me in the downwind,
a woken crow indignant at my presence;
I had happened into his dimension.
For a moment there I felt as if
the night was waiting for me
and I wished I knew the password
so that the curtain would part.
But there was only giant tree shadows
and the quiet breathing of the herd
in a snow-lonely field.

Counting Down

It was a cordial call. I had to.
"Thank you so very much…blah blah blah."
The social niceties.
But my wheezing was pronounced.
The dying winds of a fading body.
I could tell she could hear it.
Her distancing began almost from the start.
Probably unconscious.
The uncomfortable silent spaces…
No one wants a call from a dying person.
Ensnared. A reminder.
You too, will go.
How to end comfortably what began as courtesy?
A simple act of Politesse.
All was said that could be said.
Her relief was palpable.
I wonder if she even was aware of it.
That fear that binds us all.
With each day, tightening.

The Three Cats of Tobermory

What a fine pussums he was
lying in the grass the way he does
like Puss in the fable.
There was a tortie and a tuxie too
but both were nervous, they hadn't a view
hiding under the table.
But then came the sound
of an opening tuna can
and they all jumped up and ran
fast over the ground,
fearless, focused, feline,
and oblivious to man,
these three cats of Tobermory.

The Small Things

He said he loved me,
then hung his head
like a chidden child.

That darkling day
of emotions unfed
too late, the heart defiled.

So the birds sang instead
and the wind in the trees
was so wild, so wild.

The Brightness of Leaving

The halos of the street lamps
feel like final goodbyes tonight.
I sweep up the broken glass
with a certain kind of resignation,
knowing tears cannot wash away
the wounds we inflict on each other.
Burning through love's darkness
to sunrise's first light on the sea,
I see how even bitterness can glitter.

A Summer Accident

The creature,
moving too fast,
did fall.
Bobbing and bobbing
at the well-wall,
yet frantic, climbing
up and up
then dropping back
only to
dip, float, and flail
on and on to exhaustion.
Then the final thrash,
the drumming heart,
the surrender
into the folded nothing
of an empty sun, now
a floating sacrifice, obedient
to death, *maybe*
the whole agony was for this.

In Memory of W.B. Yeats

I see the sorrows on your haunted face
never knowing what they have brought for you
But the time has come, a kind of race
to put life, not death in its place
and live out your days, one by one
not with a measured gaiety
but with passion as your pace.
I see your reticence, the studied gaze
of one who's lived with emotions closely held
for whom neither love nor hate could really faze–
yet there in your eyes behind it all,
behind your gentle sigh, a call
a plea for forgiveness, for escape
from those terrible long nights and days.
So live the living, and leave the dying to the dead
love to love and be loved, raise your bowed head,
for there are those who see you thus
and dare a smile to cross your soul.

KAREN PETERSEN has published poetry, short stories, and flash both nationally and internationally. Her poems have been translated into Persian and Spanish, and she has been nominated for numerous prizes, including ten Pushcarts, and long-listed for the UK's international Bridport Prize, Forward Prize, and Australia's Peter Porter Prize. In 2022, her chapbook *Trembling*, published by Kelsay Books, won the Wil Mills Award, judged by Annie Finch, and her poem, "The Price of Love," was nominated for Best of the Net. New work is in *A New Ulster, The Wallace Stevens Journal,* and *The Cimarron Review*. Her recent chapbook, "Wamponomon: The Place of Shells," is now out, and this current release includes a letter from the President of the United States. More information can be found at: *https://karenpetersenwriter.com*

www.ingramcontent.com/pod-product-compliance
Lightning Source LLC
Chambersburg PA
CBHW030051100426
42734CB00038B/1217